BIBLE STUDY

THE RON JAMES STORY
CHOICES

"LESSONS LEARNED FROM A REPEAT OFFENDER"

Choices — Bible Study

Copyright 2018 by Ronald L. James

All rights reserved. No part of this book may be used or reproduced by any means, graphic, electronic, or mechanical, including photocopying, recording, taping or by any information storage retrieval system without the written permission of the author except in the case of brief quotations embodied in critical articles and reviews. This bible study is intended for use in partnership with the movie *Choices – Lessons Learned From A Repeat Offender*. If used as a companion to the book of the same name the sequence of events may appear in a different order. Scripture quotations are from the English Standard Version (ESV) unless stated otherwise.

ISBN: 978-1-945169-09-0

Published in Partnership with
Your Choice Publication
1245 Princess St.
York, PA 17404
717-850-3538
www.YourChoiceFoundation.org

&

Orison Publishers, Inc.
PO Box 188
Grantham, PA 17027
717-731-1405
www.OrisonPublishers.com

DEDICATION

First and foremost, I would like to dedicate this study guide to my Lord and Savior, Jesus Christ, who has given me the opportunity to speak into other's lives. I would also like to thank the hundreds of thousands of parents out there who have sons or daughters who have shared similar stories as mine. And to all of those who are searching for answers.

CONTENTS

Introduction vii
Problems 1
The Deal 3
Last Parole Visit 7
The James Family Home 9
School and Work Choices 13
Family Missteps 15
The LA Experience 17
Coke Stories 19
Coke Stories 2 21
Gypsy 23
Ron and Gypsy 25
First-Time Jailbird 27
Meeting Lindor and Finding Crack 29
Meeting Kiss 33
Second-time Jailbird 35
Clocking 37
The Road Out of (And Back to) Jail 41
Third-time Jailbird 43
A Budding Author 45
Mimi's Passing and Ron's Chance 47

Bible Study	49
An Unexpected Revelation	51
Parole Board	53
Back to the World	55
The Helpers That Came	57
Parole Free	59
Conclusion	61

INTRODUCTION

Getting involved with drugs is exactly like going down the rabbit hole; finding your way back is a great feat and you're never truly the same if and when you do get back.

This Bible Study chronicles the experiences of Ronald L. James, a recovered drug addict and alcoholic and consequently, a person of multiple incarcerations. It is based on a script for a movie about his life released in 2018.

The original movie script is retold in summary fashion in this document. Scriptural references and questions are provided to aid the reader or study group in examining the events and perhaps even applying relevant lessons to their own lives. It is the author's hope that this Bible study impacts heavily upon the reader and leaves a lasting impression.

PROBLEMS

As the movie opens, we hear sirens, gunshots and barking dogs. A man, trying to elude capture, is running for his life. He breaks into a back door of a home. Crouching down and breathing heavily from the chase, he gingerly peers out the curtained pane thinking he may be safe. Suddenly we see a shotgun pointed to the back of his head as the homeowner glaringly questions what he is doing in her home.

The scene fades away to a couple in a car outside Philadelphia. This is our protagonist, Ron James. When we meet him he is not in the best shape of his life. He used to be a good-looking smooth talker, born salesman and ladies' man. At this point, he is none of those things, just a broken man with a strong addiction. He drives a beat-up old car that would fail every test of roadworthiness. Ron doesn't care. At least the car gets him wherever he needs to be and he usually only needs to be at one place — wherever the drugs are.

Sitting beside his shaky body in the passenger seat is a woman he calls his girlfriend. Her name is Princess D. The affection they both share is mostly superficial and doesn't compare in any way to the affection they have for getting high.

As the car idles outside the home of a drug dealer, they finalize their plans to trade a new video camera for drugs since they have no money. Princess D is pleading for him to hurry as she needs her fix.

ANALYSIS

Is it fair to say that drugs degrade a person's abilities? What does the Bible share about abuse of wine? Is that applicable also to drugs? Consider Proverbs 23:29-33 which offers this insight: *"Who has wounds without cause? Who has redness of eyes? Those who tarry long over wine...when* it sparkles in the cup and goes down smoothly. In the end, it bites like a serpent and stings like an adder. Your eyes will see strange things and your heart utter perverse things". Also consider Proverbs 23: 20-21 which instructs us, "Be not among drunkards or among gluttonous eaters of meat, for the drunkard and the glutton will come to poverty, and slumber will clothe them with rags". Isaiah 42:18 reminds us to be alert, "Hear, you deaf and look, you blind, that you may see".

1. What are your thoughts on these verses regarding drunkenness and gluttony? Have you observed lives that have been harmed in this way?

2. Do you think that without their shared love of drugs, Ron and Princess D would have been friends?

3. How deeply do drugs appear to have a hold on Ron considering that he has to resort to trading electronic products to get his fix?

THE DEAL

Ron enters the drug dealer's home, carrying the concealed video camera, and is greeted by the owner, a man named Dino. He recognizes Ron and invites him to come in while asking if Ron has anything for him. Ron shows him the new video camera, which he brought along for the trade. Dino accepts the camera and wonders aloud that Ron must have a warehouse full of electronics.

As Ron walks further into the room, he sees the remnants of a drug party. Most of the people left behind, lying around the room, are still high on something, but Ron isn't too concerned with them. His focus is on the fix and he is annoyed that Dino doesn't appear ready for the quick trade.

After a brief moment of apprehension he follows Dino, as instructed, into the adjacent bedroom, to finish the deal. After fumbling around for the product, Dino claims to have forgotten something and exits the room, telling Ron to wait there. Left alone in the room Ron is almost certain he's been lured into a trap.

As he hears a crash and a scream he rushes back into the front room. Dino's men have dragged Princess D into the house and have thrown her onto the floor. Dino is nowhere to be seen. An altercation breaks out between Ron and the men but he is quickly outnumbered and overpowered. Knocking him to the ground, they continue to kick him until he is spitting blood. The door opens again. This time it's Dino and he calls off his men. Then they show Dino the treasure trove of goods they found in Ron's trunk - a briefcase filled with hundreds of checks and credit applications. Princess D cries to them not to take it, pleading that their entire lives are in there. Dino now taunts Ron and Princess D, inviting *them* to call the cops. Seemingly now irritated by their presence, he throws a bag of crack on the floor telling them to get out - that they got what they came for.

ANALYSIS:

Fools abound all around us, and we are cautioned to avoid engaging with them as it will lead to little good. Proverbs 14:7-9 tells us, *"Leave the presence of a fool, for there you do not meet words of knowledge. The wisdom of the prudent is to discern his way, but the folly of fools is deceiving"*. Proverbs 13:20-21 advises: *"Whoever walks with the wise, becomes wise, but the companion of fools will suffer harm. Disaster pursues sinners, but the righteous are rewarded with good"*.

1. What kind of relationship exists between Ron and Dino? What have you observed about this?

2. What can you infer from Dino's convenient absence as his men attacked Ron and stole the documents from the trunk of his car?

3. Think back to when Dino threw the bag of crack at Ron while he was writhing on the floor in pain. What can you deduce from this action about the way Dino regards Ron? Can you infer anything from this episode about the general relationship between drug dealers and drug addicts?

4. At one point, Dino mockingly suggests they call the police if they wish. Seeing as Dino himself is engaged in criminal behavior, do you find this ironic? Consider how the actions of both parties may be "folly of fools".

LAST PAROLE VISIT

Fifteen years later, we see Ron James in his parole officer's office as he makes his final visit. His parole officer, Rick shows him a box filled with file folders containing Ron's criminal records. Rick calls them "The Criminal Exploits of Ronald L. James."

Both men discuss some of the criminal actions detailed in those folders and then Rick pulls out the folder which intrigued him the most. It's a folder documenting Ron's violations of his current parole and it is empty. Rick shares how many of his paroles continually return to jail, yet Ron has stayed clean at last.

When Rick asks Ron how he managed to do it, the answer is simple. "Choices", Ron says. "When I make good choices I stay out of jail. When I make bad choices I go back in."

ANALYSIS:

Paul in Colossians 3:2 admonishes us to *"Set your minds on things that are above, not on things that are on earth."* He further shares we must *"put on the new self"* suggesting new behaviors and redirecting our thoughts into healthy, positive ways of thinking (verse 10). This is done by an act of will, not by wishful thinking or even just prayer. We must put old thoughts and patterns aside each and every time they revisit us - and put on the new. The more we do this the less our thoughts and actions will flow in the wrong direction. It requires setting our mind to it and following through. It requires discipline and perseverance. The rewards of Heaven are great for those who believe and trust in the Lord.

1. What do the multiple files suggest about Ron's criminal life? Why do you think Rick was so intrigued by the one

empty folder in Ron's file? Was this an example of Ron's success in "putting on a new self"?

2. Are there things in your own life that need re-directed? Read Colossians 3:12-17 and share how those verses speak to you about how we are to live?

3. Consider Proverbs 1:30-32 which says, *"They would have none of my counsel and despised all my reproof therefore they shall eat the fruit of their way, and have their fill of their own devices. For the simple are killed by their turning away, and the complacency of fools destroys them; but whoever listens to me will dwell secure".* What do these verses suggest to you?

THE JAMES FAMILY HOUSE

A flashback takes us back to the 60s, where we see the home of matriarch, Mimi James. It is evident that she is a strong, caring woman and that she showers her affection on her young son, Ron. She's also a tough woman, but early on, Ron finds a way to bypass his mother's toughness. When he is caught fighting with another boy and reprimanded, he says that he was fighting because the boy called his mother a bad name.

Ron continues to experiment with making bad choices and one day, he throws a large walnut at the head of a police officer standing a short distance away. As his friends run off, he stands his ground as the officer confronts him, announcing that he is in big trouble. Ron quickly makes another bad choice - to lie in hopes of being let off easy. He formulates a story about his mother being ill and how it would impact her health even more if he were to get into trouble. It works like a charm and Ron begins to believe that he can easily manipulate people, and as such, bypass the consequences of his actions.

Even though he is now beginning to feel invincible, a little voice, his conscience, wells up inside him, asking him what he is doing. He looks down at the cracked sidewalk and sees a small stinkbug on that sidewalk. This triggers painful memories of struggling to read aloud in front of his classmates at school. The part of the story Ron was to read mentioned a stinkbug. Ron could barely read, and as he struggled over each word the other children laughed at him. Humiliated, Ron slipped back to his seat and put his head down, vowing to never read again.

At the time, Ron doesn't realize it, but the cracked sidewalk was a metaphor for his life - a good life that he allowed bad things to take root in. Naturally, these bad things would cause a lot of damage in his life.

ANALYSIS:

The Bible suggests that the Lord will direct our path if we listen to Him. Consider Isaiah 30:21, *"And your ears shall hear a word behind you, saying, this is the way, walk in it."* Direction is always around us, but we need to be listening. Proverbs 4:18-19 states *"But the path of the righteous is like the light of dawn, which shines brighter and brighter until full day. The way of the wicked is like deep darkness; they do not know over what they stumble".* This suggests that listening to God can lead to a life that "shines brighter". What we choose to listen to can change us. We can select the advice of fools or choose wise counsel. Consider these words in Romans 10:17, *"So faith comes from hearing, and hearing through the word of Christ".*

1. What do the above verses suggest to you about the benefits of seeking out God's word?

2. Ron did not have the benefit of knowing God in his childhood or even early adult years and made numerous bad choices. How may those early experiences have shaped his thinking?

3. Ron's mother was depicted in the movie as loving and caring, yet this was not enough to keep him from making bad choices. Jeremiah 17:9 suggests that our hearts are deceitful. Ron's heart seemed to tell him he could get away with wrongdoing at an early age. What could have helped him to make different choices?

4. When the students laughed at Ron, what other action could he have taken? What would/could you have done, as Ron or as a fellow classmate or teacher?

5. What do you think about the inner voice Ron heard? The conflict between what is right and wrong. Has your inner voice or conscience ever prompted you to question your actions?

SCHOOL AND WORK CHOICES

Ron continues to hate reading, and doesn't pick up another book for 12 more years. He becomes a major manipulator. In order to pass exams in school he chooses -wrongly again - to become a master at cheating. He cheats his way through the rest of his school days, even into college, which ultimately leads to his expulsion. Ron then lands a good job working on a shipping dock, but can't let go of his cheating habit. He considers the job to be too much "work" and one day while pulling a heavy load off a truck, he falls to the ground and feigns pain in his back. As others rush to his aid, he smiles to himself, seeing that his "trick" worked. Soon he is receiving checks from workers' compensation, happy once again to have cheated the system.

ANALYSIS:

Rather than giving up reading and impacting his entire education, what other choice could Ron have made? Proverbs 29:25 says, *"The fear of man lays a snare; but whoever trusts in the Lord is safe."* The fear of what others think of you is a hidden trap, but a trap nonetheless. A relationship with Christ frees you from the need to fear what others think of you because your identity in Christ radically alters *who* you look to for approval.

1. Do you know people who depend on cheating to get ahead in any aspect of life? What are your thoughts on that? Review Psalm 10 and Psalm 14 which illustrate the blindness and short-sightedness of people who think they are invisible to God or that there is no God who will hold them accountable for their choices.

2. What have you observed about Ron's work habits? Do you think his old school habits followed him into the workplace? If so, why?

3. Proverbs 1:10-18 speaks of those who plunder and ambush the innocent, which today we might think of as deceive or steal from. It counsels us to not walk with such men as they set an ambush for their own lives. Verse 19 concludes by stating *"such are the ways of everyone who is greedy for unjust gain; it takes away life of its possessors"*. Explain what this means.

FAMILY MISSTEPS

The people in Ron's family - the men specifically - have a long-standing romance with crime and bad behavior, having taken on professions such as bank robbers, drug dealers and con-men. One of these relatives, Marvin, soon reaches out to Ron. He is Ron's cousin and he is fresh out of jail. He tells Ron that he has a great plan to make lots of cash and that they should get together to discuss this.

When they finally meet, Marvin spins a tale regarding how his brother, Tyrone, had been making millions selling drugs all over the city. He suggests that he and Ron team up and start dealing, calling it "independent capitalism."

Ron hesitates for a moment, and points out that Tyrone had eventually been gunned down at a nightclub. Marvin replies that a thing like that would never happen to them. He is confident that when they get the drugs, he and Ron will be able to move them around efficiently and that they will restore the family to its "former glory." Ron considers this, and ultimately, his answer to the offer is an affirmative yes.

ANALYSIS:

Ron's decision is a terrible one and is best described in Proverbs 13:20, *"He that walketh with wise men shall be wise: but a companion of fools shall be destroyed."*

> 1. In your opinion, was Ron limited by circumstances beyond his control, such as his upbringing or family influence for example? Mark 7:20-23 suggests that whatever a person does comes out of the heart. Circumstance may place temptations in front of us, but where do the choices we make spring from?

2. When Ron heard Marvin say on the phone that he had a plan to get them "lots of cash", should he have been wary?

3. Why do you think Ron eventually agreed to go along with Marvin's scheme?

4. Consider the words written in the book of Proverbs Chapter 7:21 which says, *"The lips of the righteous feed many, but fools die for lack of sense."* What does this suggest to you?

THE LA EXPERIENCE

Ron and Marvin take a plane to Los Angeles where Marvin has drug connections. The dealer they intend to meet has a large home and both men arrive there in a cab.

They pay cash for the drugs and the dealer shows them how to "make work" out of it. He shows them how to safely transport the stash and how to cut it so they can make even more profits. Even after cutting, they realize they would be selling the highest quality cocaine in Philadelphia. Both men are pleased with this. They plan to stay over for a few nights before their return flight.

Ron, who initially considered this dealer to be rock solid, begins to sense that something is a little off. That night, Ron is restless and hears loud static noise from the living room. Puzzled by the sound, he walks cautiously into the living room. He sees the dealer cowering in fear, watching his home security feed on a large TV screen as it frantically whips from room to room. Ron tries to ask a question but the dealer, acting terrified, hushes him.

Ron fears that someone - maybe the police - are onto them and when he asks the dealer, he again hushes Ron, whispering, "They are listening to us", as he furtively looks all around the room. Soon the dealer passes out on the sofa.

As Ron shares this strange encounter with Marvin the next morning they both realize that their dealer is also a hard core user. As they make plans to return home, Marvin shares "That's why I don't touch the product." However, Ron's curiosity is heightened and he begins to wonder about the pleasure coke users derive from using the drug. As a heavy alcohol user, he feels invincible to its effects and makes the assumption that drugs could never take a stronghold on him.

ANALYSIS:

We are admonished in Proverbs 1:10 to not engage with those who pursue evil deeds, *"My son, if sinners entice you, do not consent."* Verses 15-16 further state *"my son, do not walk in the way with them, hold back your foot from their paths, for their feet run to evil"*.

1. In your opinion, what do you think accounted for the dealer's strange behavior the night Ron found him in the living room?

2. Reflect on Marvin's comment to Ron, about never using the product. Why would Ron chose to ignore that advice?

COKE STORIES

Ron soon begins to travel to small towns to make drug deliveries. While in his hotel room, with nothing to do, he considers the packet of cocaine sitting on the night table beside the bed. He hears a tempting voice say to him, "Go ahead Ron, you can handle it. Have a little fun for once." As he picks it up, his voice of reason begins to tell him it's a bad idea. He is reminded of the side effects, which could include addiction and becoming a "dope fiend". Feeling invincible, Ron disregards this voice, telling himself that he's special and that things like addiction do not happen to people like him. He manages to convince himself of this and in the end, he snorts the packet of coke.

ANALYSIS:

Consider the following verses: Proverbs 27:12, *"The prudent sees danger and hides himself, but the simple go on and suffer for it",* and Proverbs 28:25-26, *"A greedy man stirs up strife but the one who trusts the Lord will be enriched. Whoever trusts in his own mind is a fool, but he who walks in wisdom will be delivered".*

1. What do the above verses suggest to you?

2. Do you think Ron's relationship with alcohol aided his decision to try cocaine?

3. Proverbs 25:28 compares a *"man without self-control"* to a *"city broken into and left without walls"*. Does Ron seem to be in control of his life at this point? What is driving his decisions?

COKE STORIES 2

Later that night, Ron realizes the coke packet is empty and begins to panic. It's very clear what has happened but he cannot tell Marvin that. Simply lying to Marvin is likely to not solve anything because he knew Marvin would figure out what had happened.

Ron realizes he has to come up with a foolproof story to make Marvin believe him completely. He thinks a long time before coming up with an idea. Finally, he calls Marvin. When Marvin answers, Ron shares that he's never going to believe what happened: that he "spilled the candy" on a shag carpet! A seemingly unending moment of silence passes, but in the end Marvin says, "No problem. We don't sweat the crumbs." Ron feels great that he's able to get away with the deceit and at that moment he goes officially from dealer to his own best customer.

ANALYSIS:
Proverbs 12:11-15 tells us that *"He who follows worthless pursuits lacks sense"*, that *"an evil man is ensnared by the transgression of his lips but the righteous escapes from trouble"* and that *"the way of a fool is right in his own eyes, but a wise man listens to advice."*

1. What can you surmise about how we are to conduct ourselves from reading the remaining verses of Proverbs 12?

2. What do you think about Ron's aptitude for lying? Do you think it got him out of trouble, just like he believed? Do you think it just gave him a false sense of confidence?

3. Look up Proverbs 26:23-28 and examine what it has to say about the effects of a "lying tongue".

GYPSY

In this scene, Ron and Marvin visit George to collect money owed to them. George tells them he has no money and offers to pay them some other way. He introduces them to his cousin, "Gypsy", proclaiming she can "solve all their problems." Gypsy confirms that they could help *her* make some money. When Marvin asks what kind of business she is in, she simply answers, "Profiles." This clicks with Ron, and he goes to his car to retrieve the profiles from earlier work he had done with dating services. He presents these to Gypsy, allowing her to review them. She shares she will need to do a test run; if the profiles are good, she'll pay them five hundred dollars up front.

With Marvin doubting the success of her methods, Gypsy instructs George to give him a VCR for a down payment on what he still owes. She reassures them that George will work off the balance owed them, and that she will be in touch. Ron soon discovers that Gypsy has a legendary reputation in Philadelphia as an "entrepreneur" who can sell anything she can get her hands on. However her preferred scam is to take personal information, prepare fake checks and impersonate victims long enough to withdraw funds from their bank accounts.

She is willing to teach Ron, and initially takes him on as a driver. After pulling off several jobs, Ron wants a larger role and convinces Gypsy to let him make the withdrawls. After teaching him how it works and coaching him on which type of bank teller to avoid, Gypsy allows Ron a test run. He is successful in withdrawing the funds and they continue working as a team.

ANALYSIS:

Proverbs 13:11 shares that *"wealth gained hastily will dwindle, but whoever gathers little by little will increase it"*. Proverbs 13:15-16 informs us that, *"Good sense wins favor, but the way of the treacherous is their ruin. In everything the prudent act with knowledge but a fool flaunts his folly"*.

1. It appears that even in Biblical days, crime never pays. Do you believe that remains true today?

2. Why do you think Ron got involved in the identity theft scheme? Why didn't Marvin? What factors may have driven each of their decisions?

3. Read Psalm 10:6-11. Do we see any parallels to Ron's life? Share your thoughts on this.

RON AND GYPSY

Ultimately Ron marries Gypsy with Mimi's full support of their union. Ron has an abundance of money at this point and things seem to be going well. One day, as they park their car outside their home, an acquaintance of Ron's nervously approaches them. He alerts Ron that his house has been under surveillance all week, and that even now there is a car watching him right down the street. Ron thanks him while Gypsy slips quietly into the house. Ron exits his car and begins casually walking away from the house.

At this point, the unmarked police car approaches him, and the driver calls out to Ron by name. Ron initially pretends to be someone else, but as they persist, he senses trouble and takes off running. A foot chase begins. Ron loses the officers for a few minutes, but is apprehended when he runs into a dead end.

ANALYSIS

Proverbs 13:15-16 informs us that *"good sense wins favor, but the way of the treacherous is their ruin. In everything the prudent act with knowledge, but a fool flaunts his folly"*. Again, Ron would pay the consequences for good fortune from ill gotten gain.

1. What values do you think Ron and Gypsy's marriage was based on?

2. Could overconfidence have played a role in Ron's downfall? Was it just meant to happen? Why?

3. Read Proverbs 18:11-12. Consider the statement that evil deeds are always repaid. Do you believe this to be true?

FIRST-TIME JAILBIRD

Ron lands in jail for the first time and he is stunned. Bail is denied and he doesn't get out for nine long months. He quickly learns that part of the unwritten prison code is that whoever is in the cell first makes all the rules. His cellmate promptly tells him exactly where he may and *may not* sit and sleep, and demands that he always remove his shoes while in the cell. After learning his cellmate was convicted of murder, Ron is careful to watch his every step.

Later, when Ron is released, he relishes the freedom outside of the prison walls. Soon Ron craves the high that he thought he had forgotten. Within one day of his release he turns back to crack, and as always, he needs money to fund it. His bank accounts have already been emptied by attorney fees and court costs. He rushes over to Gypsy's house and discovers Gypsy and her "people" have helped themselves to all his possessions, including his secret money stash. It is apparent that Gypsy values cocaine over her relationship with Ron. He decides he is now through with her.

Still needing money for his next high, Ron begins a new scam ripping off clothing stores with fake checks and pocketing the difference. He even returns to the same store twice, despite knowing that it is never wise to return to the scene of a crime.

ANALYSIS:
We learn in Proverbs 13: 20-21 *"whoever walks with the wise becomes wise, but the companion of fools will suffer harm. Disaster pursues sinners, but the righteous are rewarded with good"*. Ron's pattern of choices seem to always lead him in the wrong direction.

1. How difficult do you think it is to change the patterns in your life?

2. What role models did Ron have in his life that helped him choose a path in life? Do you know others who struggle in this way?

3. How do you think Ron felt upon his release when he found he had been cleaned out of all his money and possessions by his own wife?

4. Why do you think Ron once again returned to more scams? What other options might have been available to him?

MEETING LINDOR AND FINDING CRACK

Ron begins seeing a lot of women after Gypsy and becomes particularly enamored by a young girl named Lindor. She is always welcoming to Ron, and to the drugs he brings. Her specialty is cooking the powder into a rock and smoking it. She asks Ron if he's ever smoked the pipe before. When Ron remains silent, she tempts him until he agrees to try.

That was the first night Ron smoked with a glass pipe, and from that moment on that was all he ever wanted. He refers to crack as his "Maggie May" - from the lyrics of the Rod Stewart song - *"you stole my soul, and that's a pain I could live without"*. He shares how being called a crack head on the streets is ultimately hitting the bottom of the barrel, and that was exactly where he was. He had sunk to a new low.

(Though not shown in the movie, Ron began at this time to regularly visit crack houses. Nothing deterred him from patronizing them, not the numerous fights or stick-ups and surely not the several stabbings and shootings. At the crack houses, he saw people stand still for hours in a daze. Some mutilated themselves; others jumped out of windows. The crack houses smelled badly; roaches and rats were regular tenants. If you were not high, the smell could knock you out cold but Ron was such a part of the whole process that at times the smell was coming from him. Personal cleanliness, basic responsibilities to self and others, even eating, all took a back seat to the quest for another fix. It consumed all thoughts. Like many others in that situation, he only lived for that "next" high.)

Ron's crack habit needs to be fed daily, so each day he tries to find a way to get money. He begins to exchange electronics for drugs, conspires with shady store owners to get insurance money and even robs himself to get insurance payments. On one occasion he is so desperate, he puts a pair of pliers in his pocket, pretends it's a gun and robs a store for crack money. Every dollar went to the same place - to his dealer for that next fix.

The scene flashes back to the parole office, where Ron is meeting with his parole officer, Rick. He asks Ron how he could get in such a position when it was clear how drugs were destroying people every day. Ron replies that his problem was chasing the high of that first hit; though he tried many different drugs and varying amounts he was never able to replicate that first high. It was elusive yet it called to him constantly. It was a day and night struggle to fight the need for that next hit - a need that was as compelling to him as the need to *breathe*.

ANALYSIS:

Patterns are hard to break and Ron continues to make bad choices in his life. Consider this passage in Proverbs 26:11, *"Like a dog that returns to its vomit is a fool who repeats his folly"*. Yet God knows our capabilities and limits, and he is always there, if we only seek him out. In 1 Corinthians 10:13, the Bible says, *"No temptation has overtaken you that is not common to man. God is faithful, and he will not let you be tempted beyond your ability, but with the temptation he will also provide the way of escape, that you may be able to endure it"*.

   1. How do these verses suggest that God is always there? What does he ask of us?

2. Does God welcome anyone who seeks him? Would Ron be welcomed despite all his wrongdoing? What scripture supports your answer?

3. Does there seem to be a pattern or common thread in Ron's relationship with the women in his life (Princess D, Gypsy, Lindor)? Do you think this is obvious to him at this stage in his life? Are there blind spots in your life?

4. When Lindor first invited Ron to smoke, why do you think he didn't simply decline her offer? (For insight, read the book of Isaiah 44:18-20)

5. Ron tells Rick that he kept trying to replicate the high of that first hit. Could this be one reason why addictions have such a hold on individuals? What are other reasons? (Proverbs 23:31-35 addresses the fruits of addiction to alcohol. This passage is particularly relevant because the pattern is the same for other drug addictions.)

MEETING KISS

Ron begins working with a new dealer, a young, charming guy called Kiss. By this point, Ron realizes that a lot of dealers treat addicts like "sub-human garbage" but Kiss is respectful and Ron values that in him.

Very late one night, after 1:15 am, Ron finds himself in a difficult situation and calls Kiss asking him if he has a gun. Ron explains that the girl he came to the bar with has set him up and that there are guys waiting on him outside. He needs to be taken out of there fast. When Kiss pulls up in his car, he recognizes the men and knows they're not playing games. Kiss's reputation and protection allows Ron to be safely escorted to the car.

Back in the car, Kiss reflects on the events of the evening and his own risk in coming to Ron's aid. He shares his own story telling Ron that he wasn't always on the corner dealing; he once had dealers and several crack houses under him. He was even signed to a label. Eventually, his dealers got busted, his stashes robbed and he had to start hustling deals on the streets himself. He shares how ironically this all began after his mother, a former addict, "found Jesus and began to pray" for him. He started to lose everything, because in his words, "Jesus is looking out for me".

Ron tells him not to worry and that he'll bring him in on a future job. We soon learn that Ron and Kiss both end up in jail.

ANALYSIS:
Consider these passages: James 5: 16 *"Confess your faults one to another, and pray one for another, that ye may be healed. The effectual fervent prayer of a righteous man availeth much."* Proverbs 14:7-9 *"Leave the presence of a fool, for there you do not meet words of knowledge. The wisdom of the prudent is to discern his way, but the folly of fools is deceiv-*

ing." Proverbs 13:20-21 *"Whoever walks with the wise, becomes wise, but the companion of fools will suffer harm. Disaster pursues sinners, but the righteous are rewarded with good."*

1. Why would you think that drug dealers in general might treat drug users/addicts like" sub-human garbage"?

2. Kiss found irony in the fact that his world was coming apart even as his mother was holding him in prayer? Is it possible that God was beginning to work in his life? Do you know of anyone who first had to be brought to their knees before they were ready to turn to God?

SECOND-TIME JAILBIRD

The scene opens to Ron in the jail exercise yard. He notices a young new arrival and observes that he appears a little frightened in his new surroundings. Ron introduces himself to Nathaniel and offers him a few tips on survival in jail. Later back in his cell, a guard introduces Ron to his new cellmate, Dwight. As they scope each other out Dwight appears relieved to learn that Ron is not doing time for murder. Dwight boasts that he is only in jail because he got caught and that he will "do better" next time.

In a voice-over Ron shares how typical it is for inmates to say they are never coming back to prison. He shares that many will proclaim to family and friends how they have changed. Others profess to having found God, which Ron indicates was true for him. He believes he is ready to finally ready to get his life back on track.

The scene changes to Ron's release date and we see him walking out of jail. He briefly sees a vision of Maggie May waiting there for him on the corner. He hesitates for a moment, then a knowing smile creeps onto his face, and we fear he will pick up right where he left off. True to form, he returns to his lifestyle of drug use just one day after his release.

ANALYSIS:

In Proverbs 14:16 we read of the ways of the foolish and evil, *"One who is wise is cautious and turns away from evil, but a fool is reckless and careless"*. Verse 11 in the same chapter shares *"The house of the wicked will be destroyed but the tent of the upright will flourish"*. Yet, God is a God for all mankind, and desires for us to come to know him and have everlasting life. Consider *Psalm 40 1-3;* *"I waited patiently for the Lord, he inclined to me and heard my cry. He drew me up from the pit of destruction, out of the miry bog, and set my feet upon a rock, making my *steps secure. He put a new song in my mouth, a song of praise to our God. Many will see and fear and put their trust in the Lord".*

1. How might Ron have prevented falling back into addiction? How could he have "put on armor" to fight this?

2. Reflect on Dwights proclamation that he will do better next time? What do you think he means by that? What is your prediction for his success when he is released? What is your prediction for Ron?

3. Proverbs 12 compares traits of a righteous and an evil man. What do you learn from reviewing this chapter?

4. When an inmate leaves jail, consider the challenges they face with finding a meal, a job, a place to live and re-acclimating to the outside world. Would you think this is a difficult task? Are you aware of resources in your community that aid those who have dedicated themselves to living a Godly life?

CLOCKING

One of the ways Ron had obtained money for drugs is a scheme called "clocking". This involves approaching someone at a stoplight or intersection to tell a false tale of having a broken down car and needing cash for repairs.

In this scene Ron, and a colleague he introduces as his girlfriend, use this scheme not once, but twice on a trusting and naïve college coed, Sally. Initially Ron pretends to only need $40. He portrays that the money would just be a quick loan that he will *definitely* pay back.

Sally meets the need with cash, and even shares her phone number and address in case they have any further problems. Ron calls her the next day, still under a false persona and reminds her of her help the previous night. She asks if his car is now fixed. Ron indicates no, that his wallet is still halfway across town and they still need $150 more for the repairs.

Sally volunteers to loan him even more cash that he can pay back when he gets home. When Ron tries to act like he doesn't want to be a bother, Sally tells him that her daddy told her to treat people in need like they were Jesus himself. She invites Ron and his "girlfriend" to come to her dorm room to pick up the funds. On arrival he produces a fake payroll check, asking her to cash it as payment for the loan and to take the difference, because she was so nice to them. The still trusting Sally shares how that isn't necessary that she will bring the change right back to them. She leaves them in her room with her roommate as she runs off to the nearby bank.

The scene now changes to a hotel room, where Ron is experiencing a nightmarish bad "high". He is crouched in the corner of the room looking around in paranoia. He sees multiple demons in his mind and physically battles them. Later, exhausted and coming down from the drugs, he stumbles into the bathroom. The man he sees in the mirror is a mess. At the sight, Ron falls to the floor and begins to cry out to God.

Later that day, still haunted by this bad experience and feeling remorseful about how he had taken advantage of Sally, Ron calls her. He tells her his real name and confesses that he has conned her. Sally expresses confusion with his story because she believes she *was* paid back in full. Ron tells her that the check probably hasn't gone through the system, again apologizing. Somewhat shaken at the realization that her goodwill was taken for granted, and her money is now gone, Sally simply says, "May God bless you, Sir" and ends the call. The scene closes on a broken Ron looking upward.

ANALYSIS:

Proverbs 21:6 states *"the getting of treasures by a lying tongue is a fleeting vapor and a snare of death."* In 1 Peter 3:10-12 we read: *"For whoever desires to love life and see good days, let him keep his tongue from evil, and his lips from speaking deceit, let him turn away from evil and do good; let him seek peace and pursue it for the eyes of the Lord are on the righteous and his ears are open to their prayer. But the face of the Lord is against those who do evil."*

1. What did Ron experience with his "bad high"? Do you think he ever expected that?

2. When he broke down after looking at himself in the mirror, did you think this might signal the end of his addiction, or is he likely to continue using?

3. Was Ron truly remorseful about scamming Sally? Would this cause him to stop this behavior in the future? Or would this likely be short-lived?

THE ROAD OUT OF (AND BACK TO) JAIL

When Ron leaves jail this time, one of the first things he does is get married again. This time it's to the lovely Latanya Moore. Things go well for some time but Ron still has a crack habit and it affects his job, and his marriage. Ron loses his job, and later becomes enraged with Latanya when he sees her laughing on her cell phone. Thinking she is cheating on him, he uses this as an excuse to tear the house apart, take her money and then leave. From this point forward, his crack habit, once again, takes priority in his life. Even later, when Latanya is at the hospital giving birth, Ron is absent.

We next see Ron fleeing a convenience store that he just robbed. The owner races out of the store after him, firing off several shots. A bullet whizzes past Ron's ears but he manages to escape, ducking behind a car. He realizes that he is risking his life for his habit, but even that doesn't stop him from continuing to make bad choices, and ultimately he again finds himself in a courtroom.

As we hear the distinctive pound of a gavel, we see Ron being sentenced once again. His mother, Mimi, appears to be the only person there for him, and as he is led him away, in her deep sorrow, she forms the silent words "I love you".

She visits him in jail, though in ill health, and asks rhetorically where she went wrong. Ron tells her not to blame herself and apologizes for always letting her down. She tries to encourage him by telling him to keep his head up.

ANALYSIS:
Proverbs 12 informs us of the outcomes of evil yet shares the promise of the faithful. Consider verses 19-20 - *"truthful lips endure forever, but a lying*

tongue is but for a moment. Deceit is in the heart of those who devise evil, but those who plan peace have joy". Verse 21- shares that *"No ill befalls the righteous, but the wicked are filled with trouble. Lying lips are an abomination to the Lord, but those who act faithfully are his delight"*. Verse 28 offers hope in that *"In the path of righteousness is life, and in its pathway there is no death"*.

1. Do you think Latanya was aware of Ron's crack habit before she married him? How might an addiction like this impact a marriage?

2. How do you think Ron felt when that bullet whizzed by his head, narrowly missing him? Would an event like that convince you to change your ways? Why was that not sufficient to convince Ron?

3. Why do you believe Mimi was the *only* person to attend Ron's sentencing and to later visit him in jail?

4. How could Ron's imprisonment impact Mimi, Latanya, or their daughter? —

THIRD-TIME JAILBIRD

While Ron is in jail, playing chess with an inmate, a TV news report catches his attention. It details a shooting at a convenience store where the robber was shot and killed by the shopkeeper. When the front of the store is shown Ron recognizes it as one he had also robbed. He remembers how he felt when the bullet passed his ear and again realizes how lucky he was. He hears his chess partner say to him, "That could have been you."

Next we see Nathaniel, the young man Ron gave advice to on his first day in jail, stopping by Ron's cell. He invites him to a Bible Study. Ron declines, saying that he doesn't like reading, but Nathaniel presses further. Confessing that he has nothing better to do, Ron finally agrees to attend. The message is on repentance. Ron remains after the meeting, and asks the chaplain if God's grace ever runs out. The Chaplain shares it is more like a journey - you stumble and you get up. Ron shares that he has in the past found God's grace in jail, but he seems to lose it when he gets out. The Chaplain replies that God will never give up on you - the challenge is to not give up on yourself. He further instructs him "don't believe you have done anything that makes you unworthy in His eyes."

ANALYSIS:

Consider the parable in Luke 15:2-7. It tells the story of the shepherd who has lost just *one* sheep in his flock of one hundred, and his joy in finding it. Similarly there is even greater rejoicing in heaven over just one sinner who repents. In 2 Peter 1:1-11 we learn of God's great promise to us, and his instruction to *"make every effort to supplement your faith with virtue, and virtue with knowledge, and knowledge with self-control, and self-control with steadfastness, and steadfastness with godliness, and godliness with brotherly affection, and brotherly affection with love. For if these qualities are yours and are increasing, they keep you from being ineffective or unfruit-*

ful in the knowledge of our Lord Jesus Christ. For whoever lacks these qualities is so nearsighted that he is blind, having forgotten that he was cleansed from his former sins. Therefore brothers, be all the more diligent to make your calling and election sure, for if you practice these qualities you will never fall. For in this way there will be richly provided for you an entrance into the eternal kingdom of our Lord and Savior Jesus Christ".

1. How important was Nathaniel to Ron during this jail period? Do you think his outreach to invite Ron to Bible study was in any part due to Ron's helpful words to him on his first day in jail?

2. Why may Ron have initially been hesitant to attend Bible Study?

3. What kind of experience do you think Ron expected to have at Bible study? What did he actually experience?

4. What are the seven qualities God instructs us to put into practice in 2 Peter 1:1-11?

A BUDDING AUTHOR

The scene opens on a pastor congratulating a group of inmates on their graduation from a recent Bible Study. He shares that he personally corresponds with several inmates but only with those who have the will to change. He further states that in order for that change to be successful, they must first have a plan. Ron lingers to introduce himself and asks if he would write to him. The pastor agrees and they exchange contact information.

The scene moves to Ron's cell where a library cart is making its rounds. The cart attendant randomly selects a book for Ron. It happens to be a motivational book by Rob Jolles. Later Ron decides to write to the author to share what the book meant to him. His cellmate Dwight casts doubts that someone like that would ever bother with people like them.

The camera next cuts to Rob Jolles seated in his office, looking quizzically at an envelope from the Lancaster County Prison. After reading the letter, Rob decides to write back, touched by how Ron poured out his heart to him in that letter. The two men continue to exchange letters. Rob encourages Ron to write his own book, even if Ron would be the only one to ever read it.

We see Ron diligently working on his book. Seemingly frustrated at times, he plods along. Taped on the wall in his cell is the saying Mimi often recited to him: "Good, better best, may you never rest, Until the good gets better, and the better best!"

ANALYSIS:

There are numerous scriptures extolling the value of knowledge. Consider the following: Proverbs 4:7 *"The beginning of wisdom is this: Get wisdom, and whatever you get, get insight"*. Proverbs 14:7 directs us to *"Leave the presence of a fool for there you do not meet words of knowledge"*. Proverbs

18:15 states *"An intelligent heart acquires knowledge, and the ears of the wise seek knowledge"*. Proverbs 2:9-14 states that if you receive God's word *"Then you will understand righteousness and justice and equity, every good path; for wisdom will come into your heart, and knowledge will be pleasant to your soul; discretion will watch over you, understanding will guard you, delivering you from the way of evil."*

1. What do the above verses suggest to you?

2. How was reaching out to Rob Jones a life changer for Ron? Is there anyone in your life who has had a significant impact on you?

3. Is there a story inside each of us? If you were to write one about your life, what would it say?

MIMI'S PASSING AND RON'S CHANCE

While in prison, Ron receives a phone call from his brother-in-law Gee that his mother has died. While Ron struggles to process this, Gee shares that Mimi had asked that this message be passed along to Ron: "Good better best, may you never rest until the good gets better and the better best." Ron knows the words well, is overcome with the sorrow of this great loss and anger at himself for his foolish ways.

ANALYSIS:

Proverbs 13:14-15 shares that *"The teaching of the wise is a fountain of life - that one may turn away from the snares of death. Good sense wins favor, but the way of the treacherous is their ruin. Every prudent man acts with knowledge but a fool flaunts his folly".*

1. What impact do you think Mimi's death will have on Ron? Do you think he will be motivated to change now?

2. Do you think the poem Mimi always shared with him was ever relevant to Ron while she was alive? Will it have new meaning to him now?

3. Can you imagine missing a loved one's funeral, because you were incarcerated? What impact might such an event have?

BIBLE STUDY

Ron is shown on his knees, in his cell, holding his Bible. Next we see him sitting in Bible Study group considering the words of a cellmate who is sharing these verses, *"They who wait for the Lord shall renew their strength. They shall mount up with wings like eagles; they shall run and not be weary; they shall walk and not faint" (Isaiah 40:31).* The speaker shares how the chapter in Isaiah 40 sustains him.

The bible study facilitator then introduces a local congressman who is attending the Bible Study. When Ron is asked to help close the session, he nervously gets up to read. With the Chaplain's encouragement and help from Nathaniel as he struggles with a word, Ron reads aloud the scripture from Isaiah 55:6, *"Seek the Lord while he may be found; call upon him while he is near. Let the wicked forsake his way".*

This is the first time Ron has read aloud since grade school. A flashback takes us to the painful memory of his classmates laughing at his difficulty reading. The camera moves to a cracked sidewalk where we see a slowly moving stinkbug. These two images remind us not only of his early failure in reading, but of all the "cracks" in his own character where he had allowed in the past, non-productive seeds to take hold and grow. As the camera pans upward, we now see the outline of an angel in the sky, suggesting Ron's new life in Christ.

The scene returns to Ron, who completes the scripture reading. As the meeting breaks up, the inmate, who spoke during the meeting, hands Ron a book entitled *From Prison to Praise,* indicating that it had given him comfort in the past, and he hopes the same for Ron.

ANALYSIS:
2 Thessalonians 3:3 proclaims: *"But the Lord is faithful. He will establish you, and guard you against the evil one".* Genesis 50:20-21 shares, *"As

for you, you meant evil against me; but God meant it for good, to bring it about that many people should be kept alive, as they are today. So do not fear, I will provide for you and your little ones".

1. What does this scripture suggest to you?

2. What changes do you observe in Ron, since his mother has passed?

3. To what can you contribute his new interest in reading?

4. Ron is now attending Bible Study - does he seem sincere about these efforts?

AN UNEXPECTED REVELATION

Around this time, Kiss gets back in jail and finds out that Ron is there too. He traces him to the recreational room, thinking that Ron is probably running the joint. He is surprised to find Ron preaching to a group of prisoners. As the two men silently acknowledge one another, Ron continues his message. We see the impact upon Kiss. His thoughts keep turning to his mother and how she prayed endlessly on his behalf. At that very moment, from the pulpit, Ron is sharing that *"perhaps God has us right where we are supposed to be"*. As he repeats those words, we see the meaning this now holds for Kiss. There is a suggestion of new hope for his future.

ANALYSIS:

We are instructed by Proverbs 1:1-5: " *to know wisdom and instruction, to understand words of insight, to receive instruction in wise dealing, in righteousness, justice, and equity; to give prudence to the simple, knowledge and direction to the youth – Let the wise hear and increase in learning"*. 1 Peter 3:10-12 informs us that *"For whoever desires to love life and see good days, let him keep his tongue from evil and his lips from speaking deceit, let him turn away from evil and do good; let him seek peace and pursue it. For the eyes of the Lord are on the righteous and his ears are open to their prayer. But the face of the Lord is against those who do evil"*.

1. How do you think Ron may have felt, seeing Kiss touched by God's word, as he is speaking from the pulpit?

2. Does Ron seem changed at this point in his life?

3. Does it seem at this point, that both men are turning toward God?

4. What indicators do you see that may suggest how successful they will be?

PAROLE BOARD

The scene opens with Ron, still in jail, on the phone with Rob Jolles. Ron shares he has now written over 1800 pages of his story. Rob inquires about his pending parole hearing. Understanding Ron's apprehension about it, Rob encourages him by saying that if Ron simply shares with the board the man that Rob has come to know, that he can't lose.

Soon afterward, Ron enters his parole board hearing. The board opens by sharing that there is some compelling evidence in his support from a legislator, a bestselling author, and an ex-wife with whom he has a daughter. A second member of the parole board then states, "While the record shows that a great number of people are interested in this life and this case, the person we really need to hear from right now is Mr. Ron James." *(Note: the real Ron James, making a cameo appearance in the film, is the parole board member making this statement)*

Ron (the actor) then addresses the board. He explains how he wants to dedicate his life to helping others from making the same selfish and foolish decisions he has made. He shares his remorse that his current life (as a prisoner) has little value or meaning, and that he wants to use his life in a positive way. He confirms his commitment and passion to lead a life that matters and to truly make a difference.

ANALYSIS

The scripture tells us in Proverbs 21:21 that *"whoever pursues righteousness and kindness will find life, righteousness and honor"*. John 3:16 shares that God's love for us is so great that he gave us his only son, and that *"whoever believes in him should not perish but have eternal life"*. Jesus tells us in John 14:6 that *"I am the way, and the truth and the life. No one comes to the Father except through me"*. Verse 23 instructs us that: *"If anyone loves me he will keep my word, and my Father will love him, and we will come to him and make our home with him"*. Through this relationship with God we become one with him and he offers a peace like we have never known, *"Peace I leave with you; my peace I give to you. Not as the world gives do I give to you. Let not your hearts be troubled, neither let them be afraid" (John 14:27).*

1. What do you think swayed the parole board into releasing Ron? Do you agree with their decision? Why or why not?

2. Given his past record, do you think Ron will now stay clean?

3. Does God truly forgive Ron for all his past mistakes and crimes? Is this love and acceptance all encompassing and available to anyone who invites God into their hearts?

4. What does it mean to become new in Christ?

BACK TO THE WORLD

Ron, now out of jail, is working and doing well. He has a job, a car and a place to live. He learns that Kiss works in a barbershop and surprises him by stopping by. Kiss shares that he has been clean for several years now, and that he has never been the same since the day he walked in on Ron preaching that message in jail.

Sometime later, Ron has a chance encounter with his former cellmate, Dwight. He tells Ron that he now has a daughter and is preparing for her birthday party. Dwight appears to have it all together and this gives Ron hope that he will also be successful in his re-entry into the outside world. His joy for Dwight is short-lived. Watching the news later Ron sees Dwight's picture flash on his TV screen with the caption "Opioid Overdose at Daughter's Birthday Party."

ANALYSIS:
Again consider Proverbs 27:12: *"the prudent sees danger and hides himself but the simple go on and suffer for it"*, and Proverbs 28:26 *"whoever trusts in his own mind is a fool, but he who walks in wisdom will be delivered"*.

1. What do these verses suggest to you about the value of leaning upon God rather than our own understanding?

2. What factors do you think contributed to Kiss's successful adjustment and Dwight's failure?

3. Do you believe God would welcome Kiss into his kingdom with his background and history? What about Dwight? Why or why not? Can you support your argument for or against with scripture?

THE HELPERS THAT CAME

A friend invites Ron to attend a local meeting of Toastmasters. Ron agrees, and upon arrival is introduced to Dr Dilip, a personable and experienced speaker who is also a past President of Toastmasters International. He tells Ron that *everyone* has a story to tell, and that all that is needed is to invite the audience in and to share from the heart. Dr Dilip and Ron's friends encourage Ron to share his story that very evening.

A nervous Ron approaches the podium and shares the part of his life story about his addiction and his mother's love through it all. As he tells the story of Mimi and "Good Better Best", the audience listens attentively. He shares how he repeatedly let her down, even stooping so low as to steal her wedding ring for drug money. The honesty, humility and pain of his story moves the audience to tears. Ultimately, Ron concludes his message proclaiming that after twenty-five years of in-and-out of prison, he finally succeeded at staying clean and drug free! With tears streaming down his face he looks up and whispers, "I did it Mom! I love you!" The audience responds with a standing ovation.

ANALYSIS:
Let's now consider the well-known story of the prodigal son. Read Luke 15:11-32.

1. Can you make any comparisons to this parable and Ron's life? What does it suggest to you about God's love for us, even when we falter?

2. What does the parable of the prodigal son, or Ron's story about Mimi, suggest to you about the love of a parent or close loved one?

3. Is there someone in your life who has never given up on you? Or someone you turn to in times of need?

4. Is there someone *you* have never given up on? Roman's 12:12 counsels us to *"Rejoice in hope, be patient in tribulation, be constant in prayer"*.

PAROLE FREE

The scene returns to Ron and Rick in the parole office and Ron says, "That's the story, Rick." Rick shares his amazement at how it all turned out, and that someone must have really been watching over him. Ron glances upward, thinking of Mimi, and agrees.

As Ron leaves the office, he sees a brief *vision of Maggie May,* now old and haggard, beckoning him. He pauses for a moment, and chooses to ignore this with the confidence that "she" (i.e. drugs) will no longer have a hold on him. With surety and peace of mind, he walks forward to a car that is waiting for him. That car, and everything in it, represents the new life that Ron has built. At the wheel is his new wife Annie, and as the camera pans to the back seat we see their infant daughter. His drug-dependent days are over. He is now, today, a productive member of society: a dedicated Christ follower, a responsible and loving husband and father, an accomplished salesmen, businessman, author, and speaker who travels across the country with a vivid and compelling message to people, young and old.

ANALYSIS:
Remember the words of John 14:6 as Jesus says, *"I am the way, and the truth, and the life. No one comes to the father except through me"*. Earlier in John 8:12 He shares *"I am the light of the world. Whoever follows me will not walk in darkness, but will have the light of life"*. To find that light, we must make wise choices. We must recognize that patterns and habits,or even attitudes, can be constructively changed and that we can overcome defeat. God, not man alone, has the power to make deep changes within us, but we must first welcome Him into our lives, as Ron, thoroughly broken and without hope, learned to do. **What choices will you make in your life?**

1. How can we describe Mimi's love for Ron?

2. What do you think it symbolizes when Ron sees an image of Maggie May as he leaves his final parole meeting with Rick?

3. What is your prediction about how successful Ron will be in remaining drug free now?

CONCLUSION

How will the things you have learned through Ron's life impact yours?

What might you change in your life?

What choices will you make?

My struggles through the ups and downs of drug addiction were epic. The fact that I was able to make it through has a lot to do with the God-factor and I would like to make that very clear.

I have come to understand that God's purpose in my pilgrimage is to display his glory and power in bringing me through bad choice after bad choice until he got me to where I was totally captivated by him and the gospel in repentance and faith.

Did I transform myself? Definitely not. Who transformed me then? It was Jesus. It was the power of God's gospel that brought conviction and change to me. On my own, I was bound to lose the fight. All righteousness, or attempts at it, that spring from human strength is vain and will surely fail.

Suppressing evil thoughts in our hearts with determination and willpower can only take us so far. In the heat of the moment, in an unguarded situation, we can still fall to temptation. Self-discipline should not be regarded too highly, for it does not bring salvation.

The ultimate thing that guarantees a person's uplifting is a change of heart, a spiritual heart surgery, which makes a person directly in contact with the Holy Spirit and constantly in touch so that it is easier and more natural to obey and live righteously. At the end of the day, the most important "choice" I could made was unconditional surrender to Jesus by faith. He is the one responsible for the man I am today. His gospel served as the vehicle through which I learned to know him. It is my prayer that you find Jesus - if you haven't found him - and if you have, that you continue to make wise choices.

Remain blessed.

Ron L. James

AVAILABLE NOW

Retail: $23.95
ISBN: 978-1-945169-07-6

Choices is a compelling, inspirational autobiography that shares life-changing wisdom for anyone who wants to begin making better choices today. James chronicles the bad choices he made which resulted in personal cost and tragic results. His journey is a thought-provoking account beginning from a young age through his downward spiral which ultimately landed him in a nine-by-nine cell for over 25 years. James encourages and empowers others to learn from his mistakes. He challenges them to consider their choices and trust in God to experience a life greater than ever imagined. As you read *Choices*, you will discover the same truth James discovered. Choices determine destiny.

Have you ever faced a situation or a problem that was monumental in your life? Instead of running away or giving up. You make the choice to meet that challenge head-on and after countless hours and hard work, you find yourself victorious! That's what "Living in your Next Choice" is all about. It's the resolve of what life is all about after you've made a wise choice. Now! What will you do with your next Choice?

Retail: $10.95
ISBN: 978-1-945169-08-3

Choices Bible Study Available—Retail $11
Choices Workbook Available—Retail $11

NEW RELEASE

CHOICES, The Movie

Please visit our website to learn more about the movie and connect with us on social media to receive updates.

www.ChoicesMovie.com

Your Choice Foundation's goal is to enrich individuals to build on their gifts to empower others.

Please send your support for this mission to:

Your Choice Foundation
1245 W Princess St., York, PA 17404
717-850-3538
www.YourChoiceFoundation.org

www.ingramcontent.com/pod-product-compliance
Lightning Source LLC
Chambersburg PA
CBHW071541080526
44588CB00011B/1746